The
Hot Cross Buns
Book

for Viola

by Cassia Harvey

CHP174

©2006 by C. Harvey Publications All Rights Reserved.

www.charveypublications.com - print books
www.learnstrings.com - PDF downloadable books
www.harveystringarrangements.com - chamber music

1. Hot Cross Buns

2. Hot Cross Buns with Half Notes

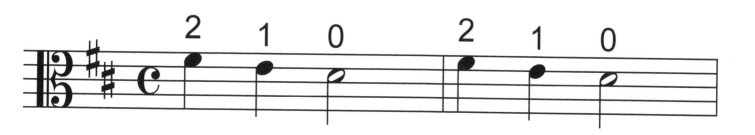

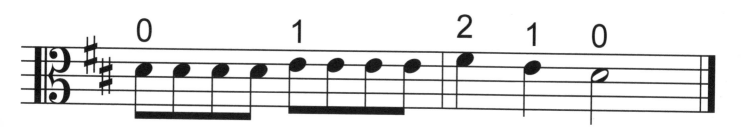

©2006 C. Harvey Publications All Rights Reserved.

3. Hot Cross Buns with Rests

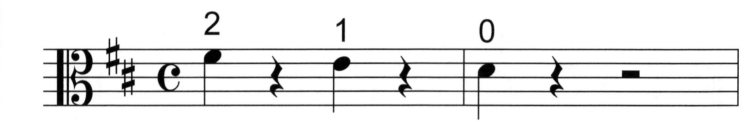

©2006 C. Harvey Publications All Rights Reserved.

4. Hot Cross Rhythm

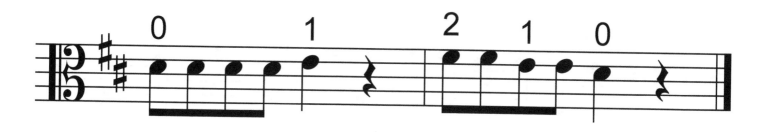

5. Hot Cross Rhythm

©2006 C. Harvey Publications All Rights Reserved.

6. Hot Cross Buns on A

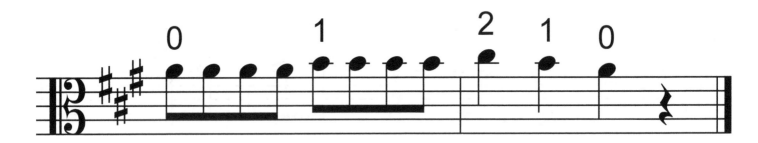

7. Hot Cross Rhythm

©2006 C. Harvey Publications All Rights Reserved.

8. Hot Cross Buns Marching

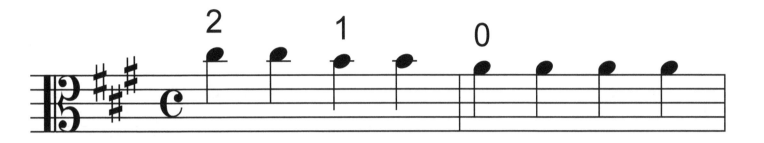

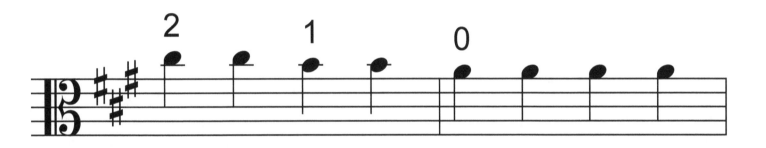

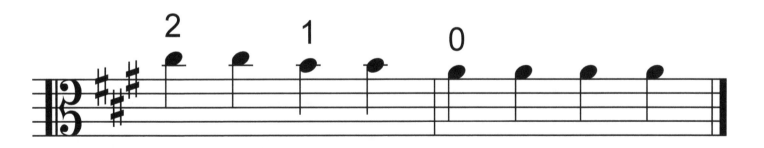

©2006 C. Harvey Publications All Rights Reserved.

9. Hot Cross Buns Running

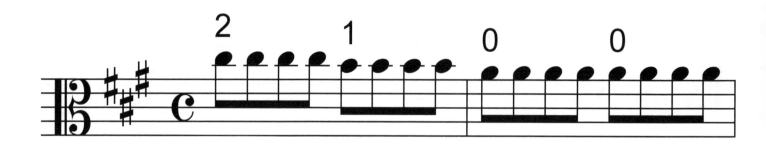

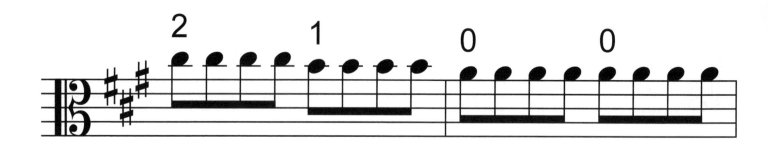

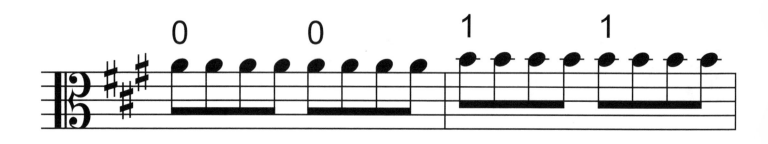

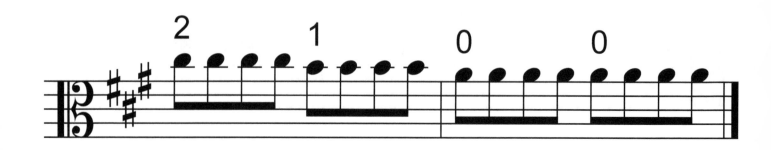

©2006 C. Harvey Publications All Rights Reserved.

10. Hot Cross Buns on G

11. Hot Cross Buns with Half Notes

©2006 C. Harvey Publications All Rights Reserved.

12. Hot Cross String Changing

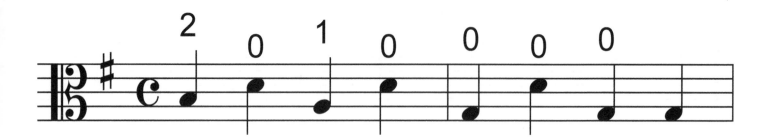

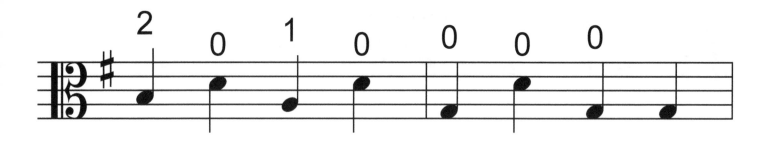

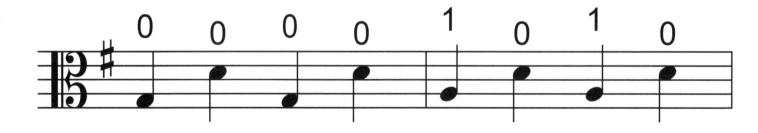

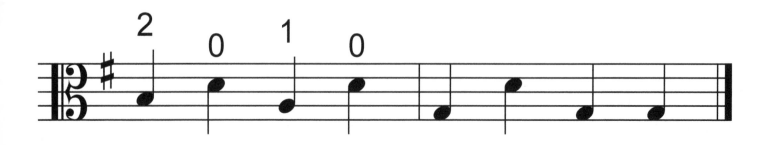

©2006 C. Harvey Publications All Rights Reserved.

13. Hot Cross Rhythm

©2006 C. Harvey Publications All Rights Reserved.

14. Hot Cross Buns on C

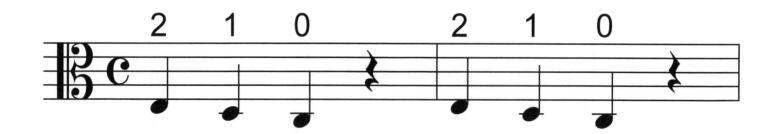

15. Hot Cross Buns with Rests

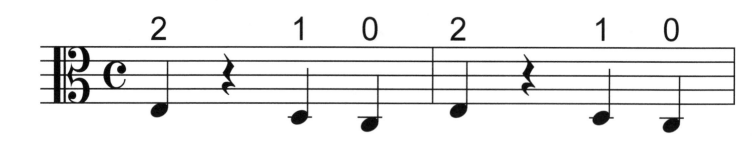

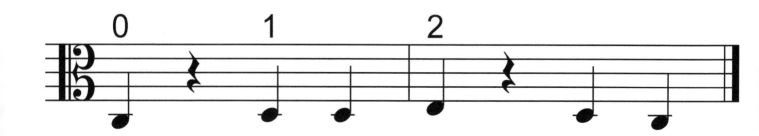

©2006 C. Harvey Publications All Rights Reserved.

16. Hot Cross Rhythm

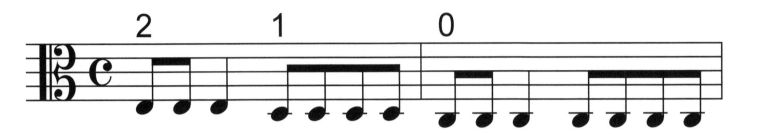

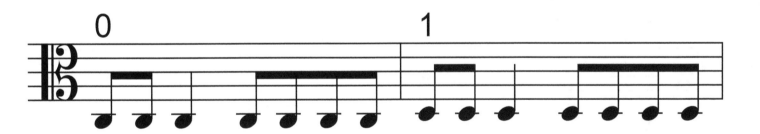

©2006 C. Harvey Publications All Rights Reserved.

17. Hot Cross String Changing

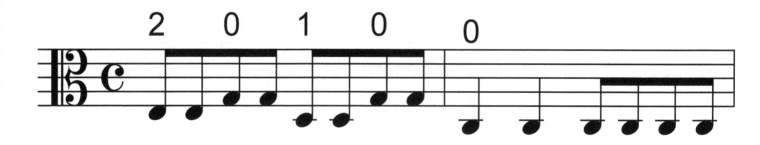

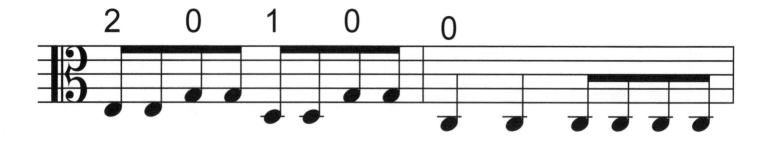

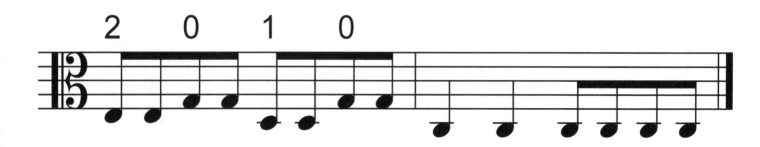

©2006 C. Harvey Publications All Rights Reserved.

18. Cold Cross Buns

19. Cold Cross Rhythm

©2006 C. Harvey Publications All Rights Reserved.

20. Cold Cross Buns on A

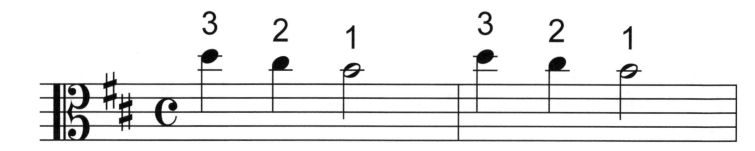

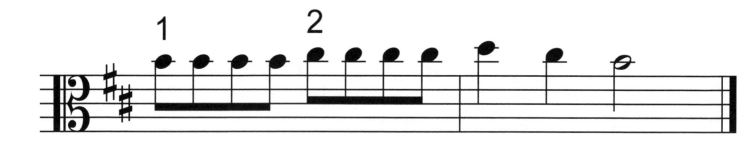

21. Cold Cross Rhythm on A

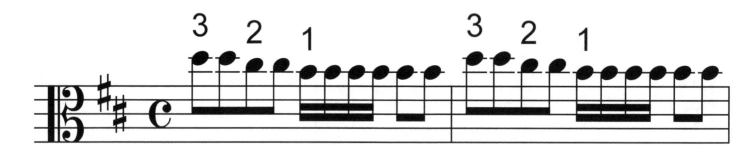

©2006 C. Harvey Publications All Rights Reserved.

22. Cold Cross Buns on G

23. Cold Cross Rhythm

©2006 C. Harvey Publications All Rights Reserved.

24. Cold Cross Buns on C

25. Cold Cross String Crossing

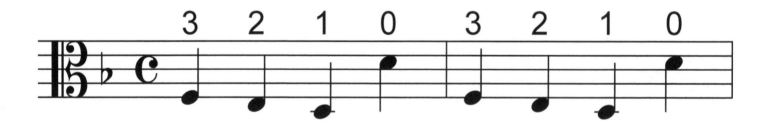

©2006 C. Harvey Publications All Rights Reserved.

26. Hot Cross Buns with First Finger

27. Hot Cross Rhythm

©2006 C. Harvey Publications All Rights Reserved.

28. Hot Cross Rhythm

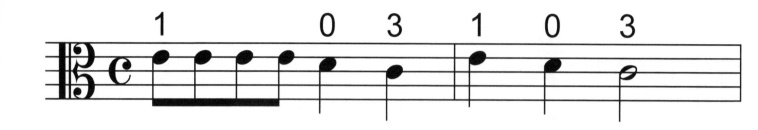

29. Hot Cross Eighth Notes

©2006 C. Harvey Publications All Rights Reserved.

30. Hot Cross Buns with First Finger

31. Hot Cross Rests and Half Notes

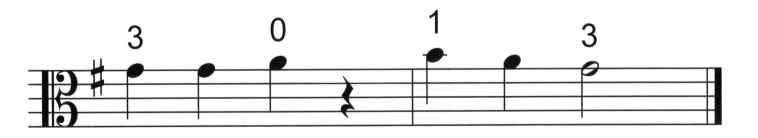

©2006 C. Harvey Publications All Rights Reserved.

32. Hot Cross Variation

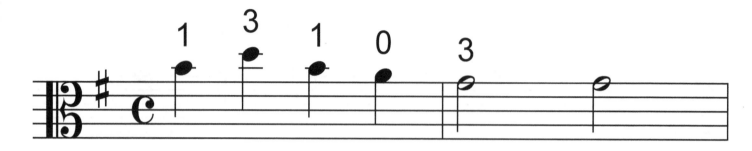

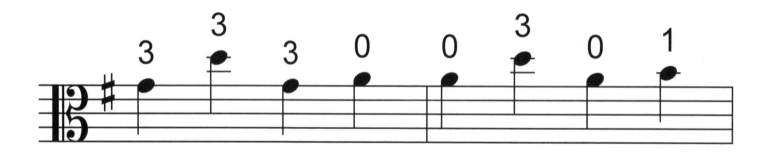

©2006 C. Harvey Publications All Rights Reserved.

33. Hot Cross Buns with First Finger

34. Hot Cross Double Stops

©2006 C. Harvey Publications All Rights Reserved.

35. Hot Cross Long-Short-Short

36. Hot Cross Rhythm

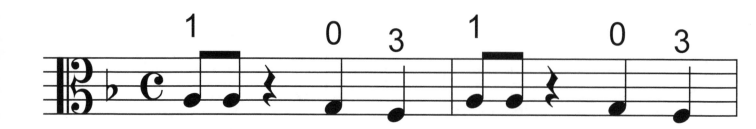

©2006 C. Harvey Publications All Rights Reserved.

37. Cold Cross Buns: Low 2nd Finger

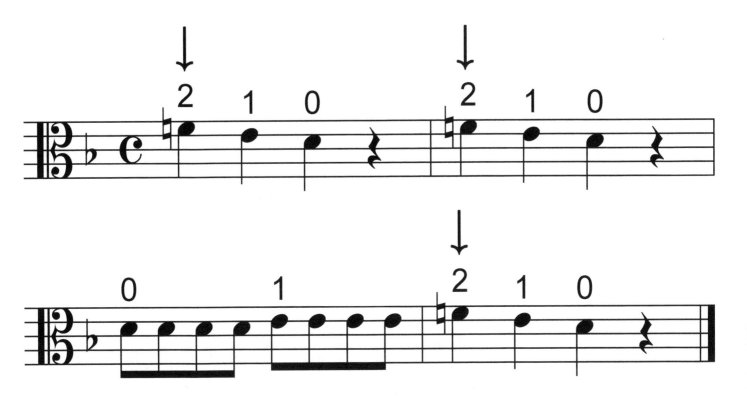

38. Cold Cross Buns Variation

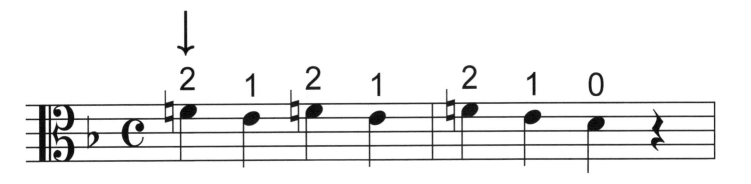

©2006 C. Harvey Publications All Rights Reserved.

39. Cold Cross Rhythm

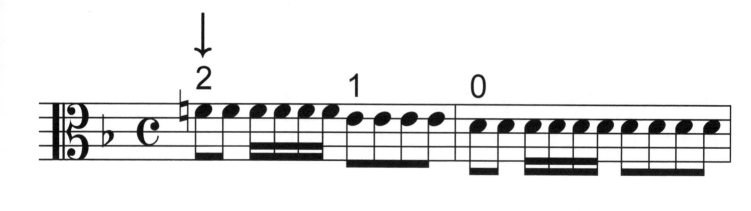

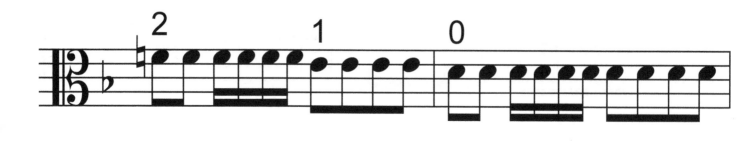

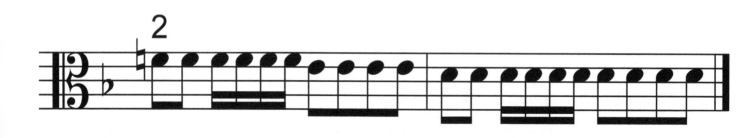

©2006 C. Harvey Publications All Rights Reserved.

40. Cold Cross Buns: Low 2nd Finger

41. Cold Cross Buns String Crossing

©2006 C. Harvey Publications All Rights Reserved.

42. Cold Cross Variation

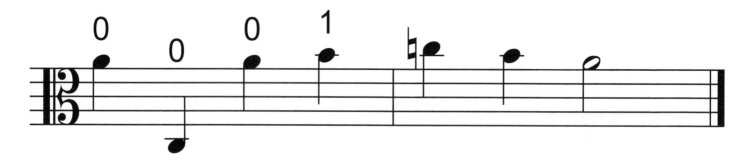

43. Cold Cross Rhythm

©2006 C. Harvey Publications All Rights Reserved.

44. Cold Cross Buns: Low 2nd Finger

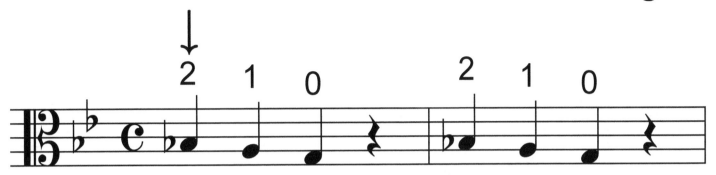

45. Cold Cross Rhythm

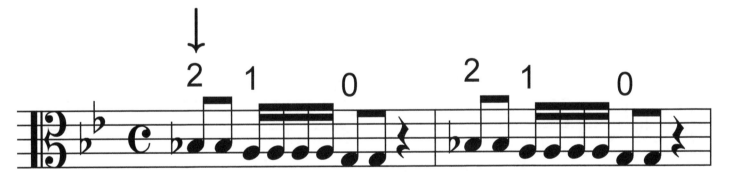

©2006 C. Harvey Publications All Rights Reserved.

46. Cold Cross Buns: Low 2nd Finger

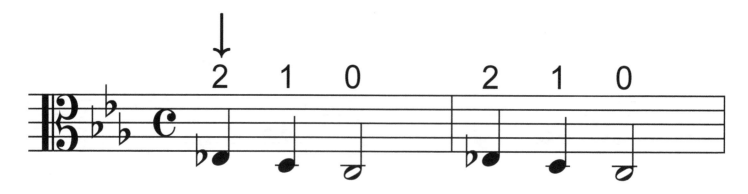

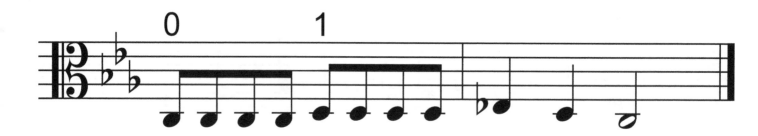

47. Cold Cross Octaves

©2006 C. Harvey Publications All Rights Reserved.

48. Hot Cross String Crossing

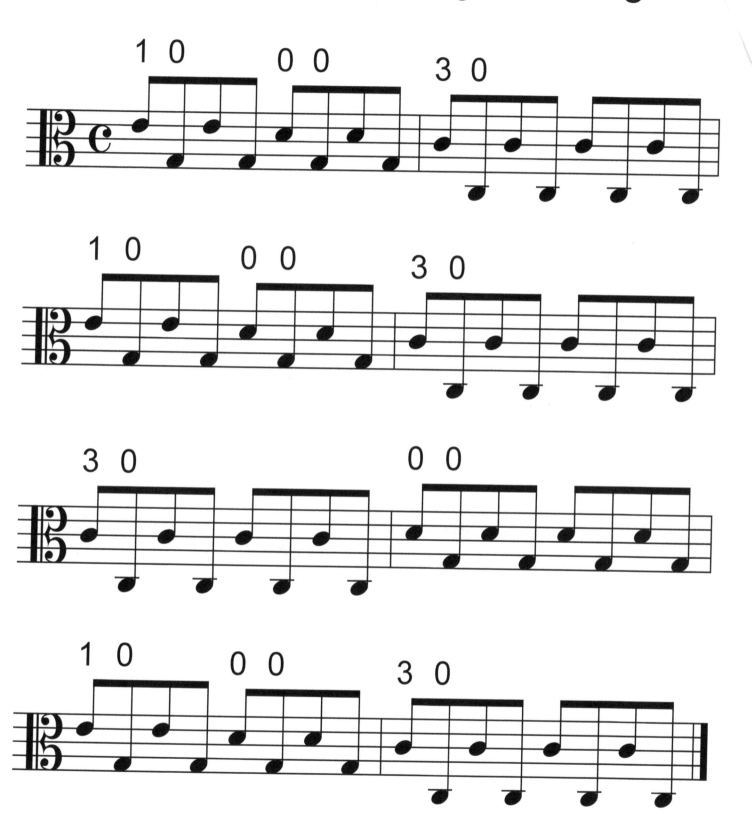

©2006 C. Harvey Publications All Rights Reserved.

49. Hot Cross First Fiddle Tune

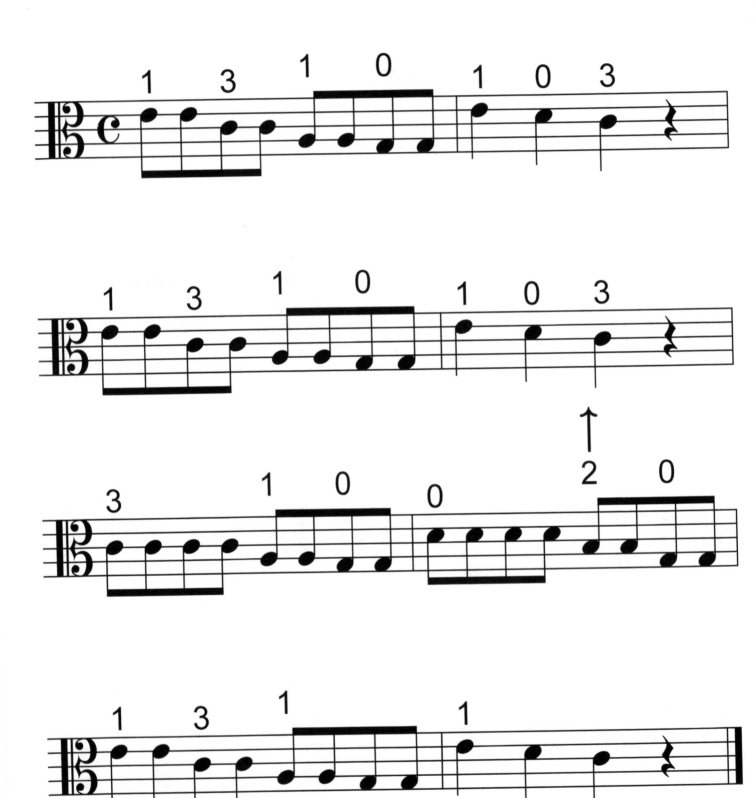

©2006 C. Harvey Publications All Rights Reserved.

50. Hot Cross Second Fiddle Tune

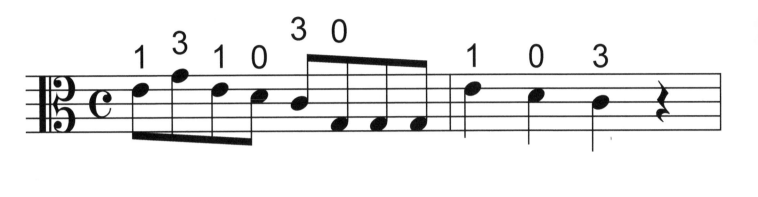

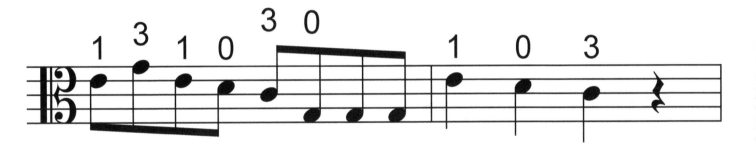

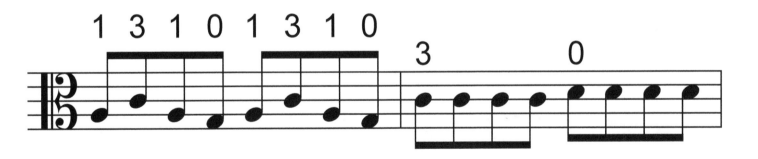

©2006 C. Harvey Publications All Rights Reserved.

available from www.charveypublications.com: CHP304

2

Beginning Fiddle Duets for Two Violas

Cripple Creek

Trad., arr. Myanna Harvey

©2016 C. Harvey Publications All Rights Reserved.

Lightning Source UK Ltd.
Milton Keynes UK
UKHW032028011022
409733UK00005B/181